Always Beginning Again...

Anne L. Lanier

Published by Arbor Books, Inc.

I0182498

Always Beginning Again...
Copyright © 2015 Anne L. Lanier
Published by Arbor Books, Inc.

For further information, please contact:
AnneLanier@aol.com

Cover photos:
Rob Dutton
www.RobDutton.com

Book design by:
Arbor Books, Inc.
19 Spear Rd., Suite 205
Ramsey, NJ 07446
www.arborbooks.com

Printed in the United States

Always Beginning Again...
Anne L. Lanier

1. Title 2. Author 3. Poetry

Library of Congress Control Number: 2014947099
ISBN: 978-0-9841992-7-3

*For all of us, especially the family and friends
of Chris Lanier, always beginning again…*

"We are like islands in the sea, separate on the surface but connected in the deep."

—William James

"Perhaps that is where our choice lies—in determining how we will meet the end of things, and how we will greet each new beginning."
—Elana K. Arnold

Other Books by Anne

Walking the Path of Grief

Like a Rose

When Time Stands Still

In the Same Boat

Just Thinking

*Sitting with the Mountain
and a Dog Named Bear*

Beginning Again...

Opening Doors

Stepping Stones

Table of Contents

Does It Matter?

Sometimes
I wonder what is real
And what is the imagination
And does it matter?
Especially when what is real
Or not
Has brought you to a place of expansion
A place of open heartedness
And truth
Does it really matter?
If you are more real
More present
More whole
If you can see through different eyes
See something bigger than yourself
Does it really matter how you got to this place
This place of wholeness
This place of love

Ordinary Things

Ordinary things
Can sometimes seem
Extraordinary
The way the water outside sparkles in the sun
The way the flowers burst with color
The way the cat curls up on your feet
Or the dog follows you to every room in the house
The sounds of the chimes tinkling in the breeze
Or water bubbling in the fountain
The hummingbird at the feeder
The softness of a wool scarf
The sweetness of honey
Ordinary things
But they seem so extraordinary
When seen through the eyes of gratitude
When seen through the eyes of time

Moments in the Garden

At the end of the day
When I sit in the garden
It seems that everything slows down
And it is these moments in the garden
That remind me
To slow down
To pay attention
To be present in my own life
To be fully here
To notice
The rootedness, the groundedness of the tree
As it reaches for the sky
To notice
How the Earth meets the sky
How the waters connect us forever
How the breath moves through our lives
How the moon and the stars light up the darkness
How life goes on
How life always goes on

When Our Cups Are Full

There are times in our lives
When we really need to rest
When the best thing to do is nurture ourselves
When we need to surrender and receive
And no matter what others say
It's OK to take time to just be
And when we take time
Just to be
We discover
What it is
To be fully here
And we discover
What it is
We are here to do
When our cups are full
And when we have had the rest we need

To Begin Again

We are always beginning again
Whether it is just beginning a new day
Or something bigger
Like a new project, a new direction, a new purpose
And if we could remember
That in every ending
There is a new beginning
Then maybe
The endings could be done with intention
The intention to end with grace
To end with ease
The intention
To begin again

Going Home

I sat with someone dying the other day
He had a faraway look in his eyes
He wants to go home, he said
He just wants to go home
He was trying to tell the ones he loves
That he is ready to leave
That he needs to
But they will not let him go
And he suffers
Because they cannot see the yearning in his eyes
Cannot just be with him
Cannot listen to his hopes and dreams
His regrets
His losses
Cannot say good-bye
Cannot be with him
As he goes home

One Heartbeat at a Time

It all begins with a heartbeat
It all ends with a heartbeat
There may be many heartbeats in between
Or there may be few
But to follow the heart
We follow our path
The one with heart
Our heart
Our passion
A life lived with kindness
With compassion
With peace
With light
One heartbeat at a time

Follow Your Heart

When you are beginning again
You can't always see clearly
You may not know which way to go
But it seems
If you follow your heart
One heartbeat at a time
One message
One sign at a time
You will find your way home
Home to yourself
Home to your dreams

Always

We are always beginning again
Always
Some things are ending
Some things are beginning
Some things are dying
Some things are being born
Just as the seasons change
We change
We learn
We grow
And then
We begin again

Every Day

Every day is a new day
A new opportunity to begin again
To make different choices perhaps
To turn around
To take some tentative steps in a new direction
To stumble and fall perhaps
But then
To shake ourselves off
Get back up
Look around
See where we've been
See where we are
See where we could go
And do it again
Begin
Begin again

Where Are You?

Where are you? she asked
Her hand gentle on my back
Her eyes imploring me to be here
To be present
And I knew it was time
Time to turn around
To listen to the echoes of my life
Time to open my heart
To see where I have landed
To see the gateway
The gateway to the rest of my life
A place of new beginnings
Where some things must die
Where some things wait to be born
A place of transition
A place filled with possibilities
A place of healing
A place of love
Where am I?
I am at the dawn of a new day
A place of light and shadow
A place where everything is welcome
The good, the bad, and the ugly
A place to let go
Ready to trust
To transmute pain
In this place of possibilities
This place of healing
This place of love
Where are you?

ANNE L. LANIER

Raining Leaves

It was raining leaves today
A reminder of the changing season
The constant circle of life
Of endings
And beginnings
Always changing
Yet the same
Sweet mystery
Raining leaves
Endings
Beginnings

The Wisdom of the Tree

Whenever I lean into a tree
I feel my heart beating
A reminder of the life force within us all
A reminder to stay grounded
And be open
And just as the tree takes what is released
Uses it
Makes life-giving oxygen
We too can give life
Take what no longer serves
What is painful or causes suffering
Alchemize it
Transmute it
Turn it into something healing
Something to give away
Something that is lifegiving

ANNE L. LANIER

Allowing It All

To have peace for ourselves
And to bring peace to others
We must open our hearts
And allow it all
The love and the hatred
The comfort and the pain
The calm and the worry
The certainty and the confusion
The security and the fear
The joy and the sadness
For it is all a part of the whole
All a part of each of us
And when we allow it all
We allow wholeness
We allow peace

The Truth of Your Life

There comes a time
In everyone's life
When you have to see your life
Really see it
With its goodness
And its troubles
And if you find it's not working
You find you have not been living your truth
Then it's time to stop
Time to turn around
Stop running from your life
Look and see what is there to see
Hear what is there to hear
Learn what is there to learn
Be with the truth of your life
Live that
Be that

The Way of Love

Someone asked today
What was my intention going forward
And what came to me
Were words from "Reflections in the Light"*
Words that reached into my darkness
Blew life onto the embers dying in my heart
"I commit to myself
I commit to love, honor, obey and cherish my own being
I promise to those I love
To do the best I can
To tell my truth
To share my feelings
To take responsibility for myself
To honor my connections…"
These words created a spark
Started the fire burning once more
Sent a warm glow through my body, mind and spirit
Said to me
Taking care of ourselves
Is taking care of the other
Is the way to love
Is the way of love

Reflections in the Light by Shakti Gawain

Our Ordinary Lives

Most of our lives are ordinary lives
We work, we play, we rest
We get confused, we think, we clarify
We suffer loss, we heal
We fall sleep, we wake up
We experience endings, we begin again
And in these ordinary lives
I see there is the sacred
There is love, gratitude, forgiveness
There is beauty
There is growth
There is grace
In our ordinary lives
There is the sacred
And in seeing the sacred in our ordinary lives
We are healed
And we heal

Bringing Peace

To be an instrument of peace
Is to live your life as a prayer
Is to practice compassion for yourself
While practicing compassion for others
Holding each other in a place of acceptance
No judgment
Accepting responsibility for ourselves
Allowing others to take responsibility for themselves
Holding the light for each other
Surrounding each other with love
This is being peace
This will bring peace to a troubled world

To Experience Life

Sometimes we find we are not really living our lives
We have stayed a little bit separate
Stayed in a place of learning
Instead of experiencing
But there comes a time
When to really live our lives
We have to put the books down
Have to stop doing what others expect of us
Stop living our lives through others
Step out and live
Open our eyes
See what is in front of us
Open our hearts
Share what we have to share
Do what has been calling to us
Be who we are meant to be
Be with those who have been waiting for us

We Are Here to Learn

It is said we are here to learn
Everything is a gift
Something to unwrap
Something to peel away the layers
Teaching us what we need to see
So we see that we all need forgiveness
We all need love
We all need compassion
Care and support
Encouragement and kindness
We all need courage and patience
We need to learn gratitude
To know we are all one
To nourish each other
To teach each other
To see the wonders of each other

Open to Healing

If someone in your life rejects you
Abandons you
It is easy to think it is about you
That you are not enough somehow
But it is really about them
For they are really rejecting some part of themselves
And so it is possible
To reject the rejection
Turn around and choose acceptance
Acceptance of your life as it is
Acceptance of yourself as you are
Not as one who is rejected
But one who has chosen life
Life without the rejection
Open to other possibilities
Open to love and compassion
Open to healing

No Mistakes

There are those who say
There are no mistakes
And when things happen that we didn't want
That we didn't ask for
Maybe the only mistake we make
Is to fail to see the lesson
To fail to learn and grow
That is the mistake
So if we could look at everything
And see the truth that is waiting to be seen
Then maybe
There would be no mistakes
Just lessons to learn
Wounds to heal
Room to grow

Each Day

Every day is an opportunity
Imagine
Each day as important
Precious
A chance to bring love and hope and peace
It is all in the choices we make
The gift of this day, any day
To make a choice
To take a chance
To change
To create
To make a difference
Every day is an opportunity
Is the opportunity

Open the Door

It's hard to see sometimes
How we stop ourselves
When we think a door is closed to us
But it is closed
Because we don't open it
And all we have to do
Is turn the handle and open it
Walk in
And when we walk in
We may find
No need to stay away
This is where we belong
Inside
The open door

Surrendering

It is so hard
When life brings things we didn't ask for
And we fight it
We resist the truth
And think this can't be happening
There must be another way
And we struggle and suffer
Until we surrender to what is
Then
No matter what it is
We are at peace
We can breathe
No need to resist
No need to struggle
Just relax
Be with what is
This too shall pass
And all will be well

Together

When things are falling apart
When something painful has happened
When things seem out of control and chaotic
Maybe the best thing to do is ask
What can we do together?
We need to connect
Be with each other
Do what needs to be done
Together
Picking up the pieces
One day at a time
Holding on
Letting go

Living in Harmony

When we come together with love
We learn to trust
Trust each other
And trust ourselves
That we have what is needed
That we can support each other
Hold each other
Hold ourselves
That we can learn from each other
And teach each other
The way to go
The way to be
And the way to be together
Living in harmony

ANNE L. LANIER

It Is Our Choice

Taking responsibility for our own life
Creating our own life
Is what we each need to do
And yet
It is hard
Life just seems to happen sometimes
Or we don't know what we want
But when we understand
That everything we need is inside of us
Then we know
It is our choice
To be open
Or not
To be present
Or not
To wait
Or not
To love
Or not
It is our choice
To live up to others' expectations
Or not

To participate
Or not
To heal
Or not
To take care of ourselves and others
Or not
To love ourselves and others
Or not
It is our choice
To be happy
Or not
To be free
Or not
To be kind
Or not
It is our choice
To be responsible for our own life
To create our own life
It is our choice
Or not

Trust

Trust is an interesting thing
For you have to trust yourself
Before you can trust others
Yet
It is the loss of trust in others
That creates loss of trust in our selves
And the only way to trust others again
Is to learn to trust yourself
And how does that happen?
It is a choice you make
Deep inside
You decide
This being is worth trusting
Is worth being seen
Is worth being heard
This being has value
Is lovable
And to survive
Must be trusted
Must be valued
Must be loved
By yourself

Just as We Are

There comes a time
In everyone's life
When it is time to let go
Let go of what no longer serves
The things that make us not enough
The things that make us small and closed
The things that make us fearful and uncertain
For we need each other
Depend on each other
To be the best we can be
To heal our wounds
And know
That we are enough
We are filled with clarity
We can be open and courageous
We are just what is needed
Just as we are

ANNE L. LANIER

The Cycle of Life

Today
I sat with someone ninety-four years old
Today
I sat with someone four weeks old
Such tenderness
Such vulnerability
Such love
One whose life is ending
One whose life is beginning
Each resting with eyes closed
The veil between the worlds almost visible
Seeing the things they need to see
Each needing warmth, love, care
Each one changing
Each one becoming
The cycle of life so clear
Beginnings
Endings
Beginnings

On Being Rejected

Someone asked me not to come back the other day
Didn't want the service I offered
Or at least
Didn't want it from me
And the pain for me was palpable, hot and searing
And I knew
This was not about the present
But feeling rejected
Cracked open a door
Behind which was much darkness for me
And this time
I opened the cracked door
Opened it wide and sat in the darkness
The tears falling like rain
Until finally there were no more
And so I sat in emptiness
And where it came from I don't know
But I was filled with love, with acceptance,
    with forgiveness
And so I sat in fullness
My cup running over
Feeling complete
Sitting in the light

Darkness into Light into Darkness

Early in the morning
Waiting and watching
Waiting as the stillness becomes movement
Waiting as the quiet becomes sound
Watching as darkness becomes the light
There is a balance, a wholeness, a healing energy
Nature knows what is needed for life
Continuous cycles of movement and stillness
Flowing from one into the other
The slow awakening
The graceful closing
Patience
Fading in
Fading out
Sacred beginnings
Healing endings

Watch for Signs of Spring

Within every experience
Lies opportunity
Opportunity to enter more fully into life
To learn and grow
Sometimes we have to wait
Be with something that has brought us to our knees
Go inside
Stay with the hurt, the pain, the fear
Stay in the darkness
Rest in the stillness
Trust this process
And just as in the winter
Watch for signs of spring
Signs of healing, of new life
Signs of beginning again

Gifts

Every experience we have
Every person we meet
Brings to us a gift
We learn and grow with every gift we open
So it seems
Every meeting is on sacred ground
Where we bring our gifts
Give and receive as we choose
Opening them with care
For within them all
Are the lessons we need
The lessons we need to heal

To Live in the Light

It seems the things we fear most
Are the things that keep us from the life we want
So that
The things we want
The things we long for
Are just beyond
What we fear
Waiting for us to heal the wounds
Break down the walls
Open the closed heart
That keeps us in the darkness
The fear of sadness that keeps us from joy
The fear of commitment
That keeps us from clarity
The fear of doubt
That keeps us from faith
The fear of intimacy
That keeps us from being one
The fear of change
That keeps us from acceptance
The fear of death
That keeps us from living
And so to live in the light
To live in fullness
We must face our fears
Find a way to heal our wounds
Break down the walls
Open our hearts

ANNE L. LANIER

Hope

There is always hope
It is always present
Even hiding within hopelessness
There is hope for what we all reach for
Hope to be seen
To be heard
Hope to be loved
To be accepted
Held
Hope to be seen as someone of value
There is always hope
Even in hopelessness

The Mirror of Our Eyes

There are times
When we look into another's eyes
And we see something of ourselves looking back
Some part of ourselves
That perhaps we do not accept
Some secret
We imagine no one else knows
Something we have tried to hide
Some falling apart
Some sadness
Some fear
And suddenly we see through the veil
See how we have tried to make everything look all right
Even though the heart is breaking
Even though things are not OK
And when we see ourselves like that
See ourselves
Reflected in the mirror of another's eyes
We might choose to stay
To look deeply
To understand
To accept
Or we might choose to turn around
Not wanting to see the truth
Not wanting to feel the pain
And the only thing to do
Is to say good-bye
Is to walk away....

Lock and Key

We all have things we are angry about
Things we are sad about
Things we go round and round about
Things we don't understand
Locked doors
Keeping us from showing up fully
Keeping us living small
Keeping us from our truth
But the truth is
Not only do we have the key
The key to open these doors
The key to letting go
We also have the lock
We have the lock
And the key
And all we really have to do
Is turn around
Open our eyes
Open our hearts
Turn the key
Hear the click
Make the shift
Open the door

What Are We Doing?

What are we doing with our lives?
If we could open our eyes to that
Wake up
Take stock
Knowing this life will end
Knowing this
What are we doing with our lives?
The only lives we have
At least
As these people
In these places
What are we doing with our lives?
Day in, day out
One season after another
Time passing us by
As we wait perhaps
Wait for "one of these days"
What are we doing with our lives?

What Is True

If we are one
And we *are* one
We have created our reality
Created it from an illusion
From a story we tell ourselves
That we are not enough
That we are alone
That we are confused
That we are not of value
And yet
It is said
Everything you are looking for is in you
Is you
So why not create a new reality
From a new story we tell ourselves
That we are enough
That we are connected
That we are clear
That we do have value
That this is reality
That this is what is true

Grace

Sometimes
When we feel confused
When we don't understand
It can be a time of grace
For in the confusion
We wait
We learn to sit with not knowing
And in the not knowing
There may be time to rest, to heal
Until it is time for answers
And then the understanding comes
The clarity
The grace of knowing
The grace of understanding

Looking Back at You

It is said that
Every relationship is related to one
The one you have with yourself
The world will just reflect it back to you
So that what is inside
Is looking back at you
So when we are ready for change
We have only to look around
See what is there
Accept it all
See what you want to keep
And what you want to let go
See it as it is
Your own creation
Your own relationship
The one only you can change
The answers are inside
Looking back at you

Don't Wait

Why is it that we wait?
And we all do it!
Wait for things to be a certain way
Wait for certain people
Wait for someone to change
Thinking then we'll be happy
It never works that way
We must learn to be happy
We must just be happy
Find it inside ourselves
Don't wait
For it is waiting for us
We need only open ourselves to it
Accept the way of our lives
And be happy

A Life That Is Real

To know that we have created the life we have
To accept that this is true
Is a difficult thing
But as soon as we can see that truth
If we are unhappy
Then we can change
Because when we see what we have done
And how we have done it
Then we can begin to see different possibilities
And we can begin
To create a different life
One that is real
Not illusion
One that speaks our truth
One that is our truth

To Matter

There was a time
I thought I didn't matter
Thought I was lost
Always lost
Wanting to make a difference
Wanting everyone to know they mattered
But then one day
I understood my yearning
It came to me
I wanted to matter
That's all
I just wanted to matter
And the truth is
We all want to matter
Matter as we are
And we do
Each of us matters
In our own way
I understand now
And the time has come
To trust this
This knowing
This understanding

ANNE L. LANIER

To Heal a Wound

We have to trust sometimes
That all we need to do
Is plant a seed
A seed of hope
A seed of love
We may not have time to nurture it
May not see it grow
But our work is done
Just by planting the seed
No more
No less
It is someone else's work
To turn around
To grow the seed
To heal the wound

To Journey

On this journey called life
There are many lessons to learn
The things we need to say yes to
The things we need to say no to
What to accept
What to change
What to start
What to finish
The doors to open
The doors to close
When to go
When to slow down
When to stop
How to let it flow
To surrender, to let go
To be
Remembering along the way
You can never lose
What belongs to you

Learning to Be

There are shields we use sometimes
Hoping to protect our hearts
We hide behind what has hurt us
With our fear, our silence, maybe our humor
We become strong, stoic, detached
We pretend it doesn't matter
Yet
The shield that protects us
If we keep holding on
It prevents our hands from opening
Our hearts begin to close
But when we surrender
Surrender to deep truth
The gift is there to receive
The wisdom
That says there is nothing to fear
Nothing to do
Just be
The pain of our lives is who we are
It is the pain and the healing
The shield and the releasing
The darkness and the light
The holding on and the letting go
That makes us who we are
All of it blending together
Creating our stories, our lives, ourselves

The Under Story

People who know about such things
Say that there are many layers of growth in the forest
And there is a layer called the understory
Where the animals find protection, safety, and resources
And it occurred to me
There is an understory where many of us live our lives
There are many layers to our stories too
But when we feel threatened
We stay where we feel protected
When we feel fear
We stay where we feel safe
And when we feel empty
We stay where we think our resources are
So that
Though we may stay safe
We may stay stuck
May not play leading roles in our own lives
May stay in the understory
Instead of being fully alive
Living in the story

Our Way Back Home

I have learned at last
That when we lose our way
We are not lost
For when we see we are on the wrong path
We can change direction
Step onto the right path again
One step at a time
Find our way
Our way to where we're going
Our way from where we've been
Our way back home

What's in Front of Us

Sometimes when we're looking for something we need
We don't see it
Even though it is right in front of us
We can't see it
We are looking through layers and layers of filters
We are hiding behind carefully constructed walls
Unable to see beyond
Unable to see what's in front of us
So maybe, just maybe
As Mark Nepo says
"If you can't see what you're looking for
See what's there"

Enough

I was taking a walk the other day
Noticing the trees and plants along the way
Some appeared healthy and strong
Others were not doing so well
And it seemed to depend
On where they were planted
Was it a place with enough light
Enough moisture, enough space?
And I thought
We are like that
Though we can transform at any time
We may not be doing so well
When the life around us doesn't give us enough
Enough love, enough care, enough light
But unlike the tree or the plant
We can get up and move
Can find what we need
Give it to ourselves
And find ways to have enough
To be enough

Let the Truth In

The filters we see through
Are sometimes so distorted
So dark
That we cannot see clearly
And so
What we think is true
Is really just a picture in our head
Something in our imagination
And even though it seems real
So very real
It is but fiction
Something made up from our perceptions
Seen through filters
That cannot tell the truth
And to see what is real
We must heal our wounds
Clean the filters
Let some light in
Let the truth in

Time to Heal

There is a saying
That "You wouldn't have been brought to this place
If you were not ready"
So it seems
That wherever you are
Is where you are meant to be
No matter the struggles
No matter the challenges
You are here
The lessons are yours
Ready or not
It is time to learn
Time to heal

A Path Back Home

To be at peace
One of our lessons
Is to learn to be with what is
For what else is there
If not what is
So to be there
To stay
To let whatever needs to be
Be
This is a path we can take
A path back home
Home to ourselves

To Risk

It's very scary sometimes
To say what needs to be said
But if we can summon the courage
Risk saying it
Sometimes what needs to be said
As hard as it is
May be just the thing
That thing that needs to be heard
And if it can be heard
Then maybe
Just maybe
Healing can begin

Acceptance

Sometimes
All we need
Is someone to accept us
Just the way we are
And to accept us
All that is needed
Is to be with us
Witness our struggles
Don't try to fix anything
Just be there
Walking beside us
Knowing we have the strength and courage
To find our way
Find our way home
To accept ourselves

Learning

If we are to be fully here
Fully alive
Fully present
We must learn to speak our truth
Leaving nothing unsaid
Nothing undone
Nothing to regret
Leaving only seeds
Seeds of growth and change
That will echo through time and space
Leaving love
Leaving peace
Leaving something of ourselves

Grace

I thought of the world
As my love*
Today
And as a gift to be received
I found myself more alive
More present
Open to receive
And the gifts were there
As they always are
But on this day
So clear, so vibrant
The cool breeze gently stroking my cheeks
The fire of the sun tenderly touching my skin
The solid ground holding me close
The blue skies bluer than ever before
The greens of the trees greener in their quiet strength
The sound of healing waters sprinkling raindrops across
    the lawn
Love
Life
Life and love
Open and receive
Grace upon grace

* *The Celtic Spirit* by Caitlin Matthews

Ashes

After a long night of sharing by the fire
The ashes lay gray and white
Looking as if there is no fire left
But stir them up a bit, poke at them
And there will be a puff of smoke
And then new flames appear
It is like that with our emotions sometimes
They are quiet in the darkness
But then something is said
Something happens
And there you are
On fire again
With anger, sadness, grief
Until once again
All is quiet
The flames extinguished
And what is left
But the warm ashes
From which the phoenix
May rise

One Story

I was floating on my back
Held up by the waters
The air warm around me
The earth holding the waters
The fire sun shining down on me
And I wondered
About my story
Our story
Because here it was
The water, the air, the earth, the fire
Holding us with love
Embracing us with light
Connecting us one to another
Making us one
One life
One story

Where Is Stillness

Where is stillness
Where is beauty
Is it in the cardinal
Calling me to keep going forward
Is it in the heron
Knee deep in the waters
Is it in the breeze
Kissing my cheeks
Or the waves
Crashing against the shore
Is it in the snake
That winds its way under the rocks
Or in the fish
Laying on the shore
Shocking to see at first
But it is food for the sea gull
Nourishment, perhaps, for its soul
Is it in the driftwood
No longer alive and vibrant
Lying still upon the sand
But still casting its sculpturelike shadow
Just as the tree beside it

Is it in the tiny ant
Crawling across my hand
Is it in the stones and rocks
Grounded, protecting the earth
Or is it the expanse of sky above me
The clouds floating by
The cold
The warmth
The wet
It is in all of these
Coming and going
Big and small
Floating, walking, crawling, slithering
Flying, gliding, sitting, lying down
Here is stillness
Here is beauty
Here is silence
It is you
It is me
It is where you are
It is where I am

Surrender

The earth opens, a sprout pushes up
A bud opens, a flower appears
A tree reaches for the sky
Its branches fill with leaves
A womb opens
A baby is born
The clouds are blown by the wind
The sun shines through
A wave crashes on the shore
And returns to the sea
The heart cracks open
We surrender and let go
Peace fills the space between us
All is calm

Something to Love

They say you don't have to do anything to be loved
Who you are does not let others down
We let ourselves down
When we cannot see that we are all one
When we cannot see that we are all connected
That we need each other
Just as we are
If we could return to each other
With love
Be love
There would be peace
There would be a place to rest
We would return to the river
Always to the river
The river of love
Life is worth the living
Go back to the river
Find something to love
There is always something to love

ANNE L. LANIER

Finding a Way

We all have things we have forgotten
Things that have happened to us
Things that we have inside of us
Strength and courage perhaps
Places to rest
Places to feel
And it is often music
That will find its way
Even in the darkest corners of our memories
Reaching in, shining light
Finding a way
To crack open the heart
Finding a way
To awaken the soul
Releasing the silence
Releasing the darkness

The Nature of Growth

The nature of change, of growth
Is the teaching of nature
And nature teaches that change is constant
Growth is always possible
Beginnings and endings
Beginning again
One season following another
The cloud becomes the rain
Becomes the cloud again
Sunrise
Sunset
Storms come, storms go
This is the nature of change
This is the nature of growth

Happiness

There is a teaching*
That there are "no conditions on happiness"
So that
There is no need to wait for happiness
It just is
If we allow it to be
If we allow ourselves to be
No need for a certain partner or job or house
No need for a certain car or accomplishment or pet
No need for someone else in our life
Or someone else to act a certain way
No
No conditions on happiness
Just accepting ourselves
As we are
Where we are
Doing what we are doing

* *No Death, No Fear* by Thich Nhat Hanh

What Waits Within

When we accept ourselves
Who we are
Where we are
Doing what we are doing
Then we have arrived
We find happiness
Right where it has always been
Within ourselves
Waiting for us
Waiting for us to come home

Where There Is Joy

I used to think
That to be joyful
You had to be really animated
Full of energy and happiness
Excited
That you couldn't be joyful
If you were quiet and calm
But now I understand
To be filled with joy
Is to be filled with appreciation
Nothing more
Nothing less
And so
Now I know
Where there is gratitude
There is joy

About the Author

Anne has been a hospice nurse for twenty years and now serves as a spiritual care counselor with hospice. She is also a hospice instructor and Life-Cycle Celebrant. She lives in Michigan with her husband, John. They have three children: Melissa, Michael, and Chris, who passed away in 2013. Anne and John enjoy their three wonderful grandchildren, Zoey, Jacob and Emily.